TRUE CONFESSIONS
HOW TO GET THE TRUTH. BOOK 1

Author: Gino Arcaro
Website: www.ginoarcaro.com
email: gino@ginoarcaro.com

All rights reserved
Copyright © Jordan Publications Inc. 2013

Jordan Publications Inc.
Canada

Editor: Matthew Dawson
Design: Shelley Palomba

Arcaro, Gino, 1957
ISBN 978-0-9916855-8-5
http://www.ginoarcaro.com
Printed in Canada

Gino Arcaro's Story

I started lifting as a dysfunctional 12-year-old, trying to overcome my obesity. Lifting tran formed my life physically and mentally. I have been lifting for over 43 consecutive years, 100% natural. I lift almost every day. It's part of who I am and it will always be, but it doesn't define me.

At 18, I started my policing career. A few years later, I became a SWAT team officer and then at the age of 26, a detective. At the same age, I accepted the head coach position at a high school, a decision that began a lengthy volunteer coaching career. I wrote my SWAT No-Huddle Offense and Defense manuals, (and recently published them) explaining the systems I had created and refined throughout 40 seasons of coaching football at the high school, college and semi-pro levels.

After 15 years, I left policing to teach law enforcement at the local college. During the next 20 years, I became a bestselling academic author, writing 6 law enforcement textbooks that are used in colleges throughout Ontario. Also during that time, I earned a Master degree, an undergraduate degree, and Level 3 NCCP Coaching certification. Then, in 2001, I opened a 24-hour gym called X Fitness Welland Inc. The gym continues to enjoy success in its second decade of operations. eXplode: The X Fitness Training System is a book I wrote that explains my workout system, based on 40+ years of lifting.

In 2010, I left teaching to make the literary transition to motivational writer. My first book, Soul of a Lifter was published in 2011. Since then, I've added several books. Blunt Talk is the name of a series I'm writing dealing with everything from fat loss to interrogation. Soul of an Entrepreneur is another series written to enlighten business owners – current and potential. In the series, 4th and Hell, I tell "David vs Goliath" tales about my Canadian club football team playing in the United States. When my first granddaughter was born, I wrote, Beauty of a Dream and the following year, I wrote Mondo piu Bello to commemorate the birth of her cousin.

I am motivated in my writing by my belief that we all have a potential soul of a lifter. We are called to lift for life. We can lift ourselves. We can lift others.

Keep lifting,
Gino Arcaro

PREFACE

I feel compelled to tell you the truth, the whole truth, before you decide to buy any more books.

1. I am not a police officer today. I got hired as a police officer three months after my 18th birthday. I resigned at the age of 33. That happened in 1990. Then I taught policing to college students, and wrote about policing, but I am not a police officer today. I need to clear that up first, before you start reading. I'm an ex-cop, not a current cop. That's the truth.
2. This is Book One of *True Confessions: How to get the Truth*. It's the first book of a series. The reason a series of books is needed is because of the extent of content. The content, in fact, is essentially limitless. One book would be the size of an encyclopedia. Dividing the content into a series of short books is the only way I know how to manage the whopping volume of material. This way, *you* can decide how much you want to buy, if anything, after you've read Book One. I don't want readers to buy a monstrous textbook at a giant price and regret it after the first chapter. When it comes down to it, Book One is an extended first chapter, so you can decide to continue buying the rest of the series or not. That's the truth.
3. Book One applies to any country on Earth, not just Canada. However, the rest of the series applies *only* to Canada. That's the truth.
4. I used to associate getting the truth exclusively to policing. After I resigned, I realized that getting the truth is the difference between winning and losing in every profession I have worked other than policing. Getting the truth is the difference between business-survival and

business-extinction. I've owned a 24-hour gym for over a decade. The difference between making it and going flat broke is the extent of honesty and dishonesty you believe and accept from customers and employees alike. The truth is the difference between first place and last place in sports. I've been a football coach for 40 seasons. Nothing is more important to building a powerhouse team than honesty – inner honesty and outer honesty. I was a college professor and coordinator in the law enforcement program for two decades. The difference between academic success and failure is the extent of truth and lies that are tolerated and rewarded. I have coached and taught thousands of students and student athletes. The battle between honesty and dishonesty is the difference between their future successes and failures. Getting the truth is not reserved only for police investigations. Getting the truth from others and *yourself* is the true difference between how much success and failure you experience by whatever definition you attach to success and failure. That's the truth.

5. Truthfully, getting the truth is not that hard. It's natural. At least it's supposed to be. Lying is unnatural. At least it's supposed to be. When the balance of nature slides to hell, hell is caused and getting the truth then becomes unnaturally difficult. Getting the truth depends on restoring a natural order. I try my hardest to deal in reality. Reality is my top writing priority. I try my hardest to not waste your time with theoretical nonsense that has zero relevance to reality. The *"X Theory of Truth"*, explained in this book, is intended to be a realistic solution to help you solve the biggest threat to organizational and personal success: dishonesty. Lying. Dishonesty will never result in success. There are no exceptions to this rule. Left unchecked, dishonesty will tear apart teams and organizations, bring down institutions, and burn up

individuals in a blaze of inner hell. This is not a sermon, it's the truth.

6. I use a lot of police references in this series only because policing is the "major leagues" of getting the truth. That doesn't mean that getting the truth in other professions or in your personal life is less important, it only means that getting the truth in policing is a professional skill. Getting the truth is up near the top of the police job description, right after saving lives. Getting the truth is what cops get paid to do. However, policing is not the only place where the truth matters. That's the truth.

INTRODUCTION

By conservative estimate, I've heard 127,575 lies during my 37- year professional career; personal life not included. I'm an expert in lies.

Fifteen years of frontline policing taught me the depth and breadth of the social disease called *lying*. Conservatively, I was lied to on average of once an hour during my 15-year police career. Forty lies per week, 2,000 lies per year = 30,000 total lies during one-and-a-half decades. I've been lied to by victims, witnesses, lawyers, co-workers, and administrators. Some lied even when they didn't have to. Suspects were different, since some lied, but eventually many confessed the truth.

Forty seasons of football coaching taught me next-level competitive lying. Players lie. Fellow staff members lie. Administrators lie. The volume of lies increases proportionately with the level of play. High school football liars are beginners. Lies get more advanced at the collegiate and semi-pro levels. Conservatively, I am lied to an average of once per day during the season, and much more in the off-season, where potential recruits lie as if it's their calling. They lie about a wide range of issues such as strength training achievements, intention to try-out for my team, academic marks, and track records. These recruits are truly revisionist historians. An estimated three hundred sixty-five lies per year = a total of 12,775 lies over three decades of my coaching career, and still counting.

Twenty years of teaching and coordinating community college law-enforcement programs taught me the extent of academic liars. Students lie. Co-workers lie. Teaching applicants lie at job interviews. Administrators lie. Conservatively, I was lied to about twice an hour, 16 lies per day, 64 lies per week, resulting in 3,200 lies annually. Total college-era lies are an estimated 64,000.

Eleven years as a gym owner taught me about the business of lying. Employees lie. Customers lie. Job applicants really lie. A business owner hears superset lies; back-to-back lies with no rest in between. At an average of 40 lies per week, I've been lied to about 20,800 times trying to survive in business over a decade, and still counting.

There are two primary reasons for widespread compulsive lying. It's easy and it's rewarded. Lying is widely perceived to be effortless, painless, and the quickest as well as best solution to all problems. The reason for this belief is arrogance or ignorance. Those who lie to you believe that you are gullible and stupid enough to believe any bullshit, or that you are too lazy or too fearful to challenge their lies. Eventually, compulsive lying is hardwired in the liar by the strongest reinforcement of all: zero consequences. Supported lying turns amateur liars into professional liars. Getting the truth from a professional liar takes hard work.

The difference between success and failure by whatever definition you attach to either, in any profession and any organization, is the extent of honesty and dishonesty. Truth and lies are the true difference between winning and losing in any career or on any team. What is believed and what is not believed determines direction. The objective is to believe honesty and disbelieve dishonesty. Not vice-versa. However, there are two main problems with believing and disbelieving:

i. Truth and lies have similar DNA – words.
ii. Evaluating credibility depends on word processing, that is, human opinion. Word processing is complicated and flawed. It lacks scientific precision. There are countless variables that affect what we believe and disbelieve, and whether or not we are being lied to. Without putting effort into it, scoring a person's credibility can become guesswork.

The main reason I quit policing after 15 years was that I got kicked out of the detective office after 6 years and sent back to uniform patrol. I couldn't do it. I didn't want to do it. No disrespect to uniform patrol, but I had spent almost a decade wearing a uniform. I needed a new challenge. Detective work gave me that challenge, the challenge of getting the truth; the truth from offenders, from witnesses, and from victims. There was no greater challenge than getting a true confession and developing a network of informants. When that challenge was gone, so was I.

I was taught rules of evidence as a police officer, but I wasn't taught the theory of getting the truth. So, I became self-taught. The psychology of true confessions is not a popular academic subject. There's a scarcity of literature written about how to get the truth. After I left policing, I taught the theory of true confessions to college students in my investigation classes, because getting the truth has always been, and will always be, one of the biggest investigative challenges. Today, there's still not a lot of hardcore literature about interview/interrogation training.

Learning to get the truth doesn't just happen. Nothing just happens. A lot of training and practical experience is needed to develop expertise. When I was a detective, I was taught a simple investigative mindset to solve the most crime in the least time:

i. Get a confession for the original crime – get the suspect to *truthfully confess* to the original crime.
ii. Get confessions for unrelated crimes committed.
iii. Get information about who committed other crimes.

After the suspect has confessed to the current crime, get him to confess to all his past unsolved crimes. Then, turn him into a confidential informant. Get him to rat out. Get as much information as possible about other crimes, especially, confessions made to suspects by other suspects.

Three steps to high-speed high-volume crime-solving. The motivation was simple: *you're working for the victim*. The victim was the central focus. The victim must never be forgotten; past, present, and future. Preventing *future* victims was as high a priority as working for the *current* victim.

Unsolved crime was failure. Not getting a true confession was failure. Not turning the guy into an informant was failure. Three forms of failure, and they're all connected. That was the policing culture I worked in. It was simple, and no-nonsense. You either did your job, or you failed to do it. There was nothing in between. Additionally, there was no such thing as tenure. After 9 years of uniform, I was given a 6-month probationary detective assignment, and at the end of that time period, my probation was lifted, but only in theory. I always believed I was one messed-up, failed investigation away from going back to uniform.

I had three incredible mentors in the detective office who challenged me with the exact same objectives: Get suspects to talk – about themselves and others. Get confessions, then, get them to turn. It was a three-step process that was emphasized over and over. My focus never changed: Confess to the crime, confess to more crimes, and implicate others.

My motivation for this book? *The victim.*

CHAPTER 1

CASE STUDY #1

My daughter was in elementary school in a different city from where I worked as a detective. One day, she told me a story about an incident that had happened the previous day: She walked home from school for lunch. Her friends walked with her until the last 2 blocks before home. As she passed by another elementary school (that she didn't attend), alone, a man in a parked car yelled to her, *"Hey, do you know where the Centennial Pool is?"* My daughter ignored him, and ran the two blocks to our house. Inexplicably, she waited 24 hours to tell me.

My daughter described the man as about 30 years old with long dark hair and a beard. She described the car as being blue with a "shiny piece" separating the driver's door and rear passenger door, "just like Nonno's car."

Blood is not only thicker than water, it can boil faster.

Evaluating witness credibility is not easy. There is no statute in Canadian law that explains concrete guidelines about evaluating witness credibility – adults or children. Some guidelines are scattered in case law, but you have to invest the time and energy to research them. I was never trained exactly how to do it. I was never taught a concrete way of figuring out what to believe, what not to believe, and why. So I came up with my own system. After I left policing, I taught it, and got it published. But it's not scientific. Regardless, I believed my daughter, and conducted an investigation.

I went to the police station, just a few blocks from my daughter's school, to find out if there were any past similar incidents. There were. Plenty. There was a long list of unsolved incidents. I next went door-to-door, canvassing the neighbourhood around the 2 elementary schools. I heard about more incidents, many previously unreported. In cases where a vehicle was identified, by licence number or description, it was the same vehicle each time, leading me to conclude that it was the same person in all incidents; some involved the offense of Indecent Act, and some involved asking children for directions to the Centennial Pool.

The problem? Every Indecent Act offence had been committed outside the six-month time limit, and the suspect's signature line, asking for directions to the Centennial Pool, constituted no offence at that time, because the offence of Criminal Harassment was not enacted until several years later.

Thus, there was nothing to charge the suspect with. No authority to arrest. I couldn't prove any sort of identity. And, the suspect had never been interviewed or questioned. The first complaint happened five years before my daughter's complaint, but no one had ever asked a suspect a single question. No one even tried to get the truth.

I had only one call to make. One choice. One investigative strategy.

The vehicle was registered to a woman with twin sons. I went to the home of the registered owner of the vehicle at 1:00 pm one day. The woman told me that both her twin sons were working. I wrote a note and asked her to give it to her sons. Here's what I wrote:

> *"Whoever scared my daughter the other day at noon, come to the police station, and tell them to call me. Signed – Detective Arcaro, victim's dad."*

I got a phone call at 4:30 pm that same day from the police station telling me that a man was at the front desk with a note, asking to talk to me. When I arrived, the suspect identified himself (as one of the twins). He consented to questioning. I told him he was not under arrest, and was free to leave at any time. He was extremely cooperative. He not only consented to questioning, he was *eager* to be questioned.

I stuck to two themes:
    i. Incident narratives (from the victims' perspective). I explained the full extent of the harm done to the victims by focusing directly on what the victims experienced.

  ii. Asking for reasons. *"Why* did you do it?" not *"Did* you do it?"

  There was no yelling, no threats, and no violence. I never raised my voice. There was no script; I spoke straight from the heart. He confessed in less than 15 minutes. *"Got a problem. I need help."* It was one of the quickest confessions I ever got. He admitted to all incidents over five years. Then, he voluntarily admitted himself into the psychiatric ward under the Mental Health Act.

  I completed the report and, in the process, cleared over 30 occurrences. They went into the system, and got signed all the way through. The guy never re-offended. I never asked why no one bothered to question the suspect for five years.

Lessons learned:

1. *Make a call and stick to it.* Evaluate the evidence and decide on a game plan before you start the interview.
2. *Strategize & improvise.* Scripts don't work. Inflexible dialogue is disingenuous and ineffective. Make a general dialogue plan, but adapt to the specific responses or silence from the suspect.
3. *Speak straight from the heart.* True self gets a true confession.
4. *Honesty out, honest in.* No tricks, no gimmicks, and no bullshit.

Cognitive Dissonance

  Leon Festinger, a social psychologist, pioneered the theoretical concept of cognitive dissonance.[1] By definition, cognitive dissonance is an uncomfortable, unpleasant inner conflict caused by an individual's *perceived* inconsistencies between personal beliefs and actions. Contradicting conduct causes cognitive dissonance. When we do anything that contradicts our personal beliefs, we start feeling like hell, and eventually burn up if nothing is done to solve it.

---

[1] Leon Festinger (1957). A theory of cognitive dissonance. Evanston, IL: Row, Peterson.

Here's the key point: cognitive dissonance is personal. Customized. Tailor-made. You suffer cognitive dissonance when *you* do anything that you believe is wrong. Many wrongs are no-brainers, universally accepted as wrong. Others are not. Cognitive dissonance is connected directly to your right-from-wrong belief. How much inner hell you feel depends on your definition of what the admission standards are for hell.

There are only 2 ways to deal with the psychological pain of cognitive dissonance: mask the pain with rationalization, or cure it with reconciliation. Only one results in a true confession.

Cognitive dissonance is a powerful motivator. The compulsion to confess is the truth switch. Once the switch is on, the truth pours out, resulting in the best evidence possible: a self-generated true confession. From an interviewer's point-of-view, cognitive dissonance is the biggest truth-seeking advantage. Cognitive dissonance applies legal, ethical pressure on the suspect. It starts the ball rolling toward the truth. Select your words carefully, and you will have a natural partner *inside* the suspect. Cognitive dissonance always works in the interviewer's favour.

Everyone has a conscience. No exceptions. If you're alive, you have a conscience. The myth of "no conscience" actually means weak or dysfunctional conscience. Strength levels vary considerably from powerful to weak; functional to dysfunctional. The good news is that any conscience can be strengthened. The bad news is that any conscience can be weakened. Like muscles, you can build up a conscience, or tear it down.

A strong conscience is your best partner. Dual meaning: The suspect's and yours. A strong conscience can't be beat, because it activates the compulsion to confess. The inner hell of guilt activates the compulsion to confess through the conscience. Inner conflict is psychological pain that needs relief. You can't hide from inner demons; they have to be released. The power of a strong conscience has limitless lifting capacity. A strong conscience can lift a weak conscience.

Appealing to the conscience is the true secret to true confessions. It is the true secret, but doing it is easier said than done. Appealing to the conscience doesn't just happen. There's no direct route. You have to find it in each and every case. Appealing to the conscience means *make the conscience functional and work.* Triple meaning: make it work out, make it work right, and make it do all the work.

Appealing to the conscience is a psychological process that involves word processing. The biggest challenge in appealing to the conscience is the mechanism of words. The only way that words get through to the conscience is by processing. However, word processing is not created equal. Every human has a unique word processor. That's why there's no fool-proof generic way that guarantees words will successfully appeal to a conscience.

Appealing to the conscience depends on the interest-rate. The difference between hiding the truth and revealing the truth is the interest rate. Deciding which direction to take at the cognitive dissonance crossroads depends on where the focus is – on self-interest or on outside-interest. High self-interest rate hides the truth. Low self-interest rate reveals the truth. Outside-interest is the investment with the highest return. The best way to appeal to any conscience is to change the interest-rate. If you change the focus, you also change the outcome. Focus on outside interest. Don't focus on negative self-interest; not yours or the suspect's.

True confessions are the best evidence in any case. A true confession proves an entire case, all of it. But, not all true confessions are automatically admissible. True confessions to persons-*not*-in-authority, for example, a friend, are automatically admissible without a voir dire: a trial within a trial that determines admissibility. True confessions to persons-*in*-authority, for example, a police officer, are not automatically admissible – a voir dire is needed. Either way, no evidence is stronger than a true confession. No exceptions.

Acknowledging moral wrong doing causes trouble for the soul. Getting at the truth involves *soul-searching*. The most challenging search is the quest for moral character. A successful soul-searching depends on perspective of *wrong*. How *wrong* is classified determines whether truth is revealed or concealed.

A true confession heals a troubled soul. The fight for the soul is the reason why interviewing and interrogation is so difficult. Unresolved conflict, inner and outer, is the cause of all hell. The good news is that reconciliation fixes what's broken inside. It's the solution. The bad news is that reconciliation is not the obvious choice. It gets obscured in a large menu of alternatives. It often drops in the standings of priorities, sometimes to dead last. The key is to push reconciliation to the top of the list. Force a *performance demand*. A self-generated performance demand is key to making the best choice, a confession, a no-brainer.

Not trying is inexcusable. Interviewing doesn't require heavy lifting. Asking questions doesn't take back-breaking physical exertion. There are no negatives to at least trying to interview a suspect. In the preceding Case Study involving my daughter, it took five years for the suspect to be asked anything. Who knows how much could have been prevented if he had been questioned earlier. Not trying to get a true confession from a suspect is baffling.

There's no excuse for not interviewing a suspect. There's no excuse for not trying to get the truth. In the most important case of my career, one that proved to be a turning point from being a rookie detective, I didn't interview a suspect who was being investigated for putting a contract on a cop's life.

Here are the links to the inquiry of the NRP Service that resulted from the case (amongst other incidents) if you'd like to read further.

TRUE CONFESSIONS

http://archive.org/stream/reportofniagarar00roya/reportofniagarar00roya_djvu.txt

http://prod.library.utoronto.ca/datalib/data/utm/nrpf_90/05-30-90.2

http://prod.library.utoronto.ca/datalib/data/utm/nrpf_90/08-15-90.209

∞

CHAPTER 2
Language of the Truth

Getting the truth has its own language. The language of the truth is divided into two parts:

i. *Vocabulary.* The *X Theory of Truth* has its own dictionary; a glossary of words and terms.

ii. *Communication.* What to say to get the truth. Content of speech and speech pattern.

Book One explains only the *vocabulary*. The *communication* strategy, a lengthy topic, will be explained in the rest of the series.

VOCABULARY

Cognitive dissonance: Mental conflict. Tension caused by self-contradiction. Not acting in accordance with self-beliefs. The guilt of doing what is personally believed to be wrong.

High cognitive dissonance: One type of inner conflict and guilt generated by an intense focus on the consequences suffered by victims and anyone else other than the offender. High cognitive dissonance is represented at the top of the X by V-gap.

Low cognitive dissonance: One type of inner conflict and guilt generated by an intense focus on personal consequences and personal suffering. Low cognitive dissonance is represented at the bottom of the X by A-gap.

Conscience: Inner voice that judges performance and scores moral character, informing us as to how well we are distinguishing right from wrong.

Compulsion to confess: The conscience's inner demand to tell the truth in order to resolve cognitive dissonance.

Compulsion to rationalize: The mind's inner demand to lie, deny, and make alibis to resolve cognitive dissonance by justifying the wrongdoing.

High self-interest: Extreme selfishness that focuses on the personal consequences and personal suffering.

Low self-interest: Extreme unselfishness that focuses on the consequences suffered by others for a personal wrongdoing.

Morally wrong: An offender's belief that his/her wrongdoing primarily hurts someone else.

Selfishly wrong: An offender's belief that his/her wrongdoing primarily hurts him/her the most (not the victim).

Free will: Discretion; the freedom to make choices, that is, voluntary decision-making.

Binding the conscience: Giving the conscience only one decision to make.

Self-generated performance demand: An order issued by the mind. There is no choice in the matter; no alternative, and no escape.

True confession: A true admission of guilt.

False confession: A fabricated admission of guilt brought on by extreme coercion.

Self-generated confession: A voluntary true confession induced by the offender's conscience, not by external inducement which may include threats, violence or promises.

Alignment: Inner peace. A guilt-free feeling. Beliefs and conduct match. They line up in harmony.

∞

CHAPTER 3
X Theory of Truth

The *X Theory of Truth* is based on one fundamental concept: *make the conscience work*. Triple meaning: make it work out, make it work right, and make it do all the work. Strengthen the conscience, use its strength to execute flawlessly, and let a strong conscience do all the heavy lifting. Let the conscience lift the heavy weight of *guilt*.

The *X Theory of Truth* is a system that *naturally* reveals the truth; truth is a natural psychological outcome. Humans have a natural inner drive to tell the truth. The drive is fueled by a need for inner peace, a feeling of guilt-free inner harmony achieved when actions align with moral beliefs.

Here's how the *X Theory of Truth* works; the X has two primary features:
i. Two gaps, one at the top of the X, and another at the bottom.
ii. The Crossroad, that is, the middle of the X.

The top half of the X is the upright V-shape. The top gap between the upright V-shape has an informal name and a formal name. The formal name is *high cognitive dissonance gap*. The shorter, informal name that simplifies it is *V-gap*.

The lower half of the X is the inverted V-shape. The bottom gap between the inverted V-shape has an informal and formal name as well. The formal name is *low cognitive dissonance gap*. The shorter, informal name that simplifies it is *A-gap*.

Both V-gap and A-gap share almost identical DNA…except for one difference.

Both gaps represent cognitive dissonance; inner conflict felt by acting contrary to personal beliefs. Guilt caused by acknowledged wrongdoing. Both gaps also represent the separation between action and belief: The greater the wrongdoing, the wider the gap, the wider the gap, the worse the guilt. The *only* difference between the V-gap and the A-gap is the focus of the consequence and suffering.

V-gap guilt focuses on low self-interest. The offender believes someone else is suffering the worst consequence because of the wrong doing. A-gap guilt focuses on high self-interest. The offender believes s/he will suffer the worst consequence of his/her wrongdoing. Both gaps cause the inner hell of cognitive dissonance that needs to be resolved and relieved, but the resolution and relief take different paths to the Crossroad at the middle of the X.

The only way to resolve and relieve either type of cognitive dissonance is to *close the gap*. Closing the gap means making actions and beliefs cross paths. An alignment needs to be made. When actions and beliefs cross paths at the Crossroad in the middle of the X, the offender feels guilt-free. He/she obtains inner peace; balance and harmony.

There are two different paths to the Crossroad: true confession, or rationalization. True confession is reconciliation; true admission of guilt. Rationalization is deception; lies, alibis, and denials. Both true confession and rationalization lead to the same place: the Crossroad at the middle of the X. Both result in the same outcome: guilt-free inner peace. The difference is the duration of the inner peace. True confession is permanent in relation to that wrongdoing. The guilt about that sin is erased. Rationalization is not recognized by the conscience as a long-term solution. Justifying wrong with the delusion of excuses creates a false reality that masks the pain, hiding it but not curing it. Guilt will return when the focus changes to low self-interest. The past will come back to haunt when the offender thinks of the victim's suffering. Only the truth can truly set us free.

Every human has a conscience. No exception.

Yet, consciences are not created equal. Some are strong, and others are weak, i.e., functional or dysfunctional. A strong, functional conscience activates the compulsion to confess. Guaranteed. A weak, dysfunctional conscience won't activate the compulsion to confess. Instead, it activates the compulsion to rationalize. Guaranteed. Rationalization lowers an individual's moral beliefs and moral standards, making it easier to re-offend. True confession raises the bar, lifting moral beliefs and moral standards. Re-offending won't be easy.

True confession happens when high cognitive dissonance is strong enough for the conscience to activate the compulsion to confess. The compulsion to confess is a natural "use of force" tactic; a force of nature where the confession is voluntarily made because of a self-generated performance demand to talk; to clear one's conscience by admitting guilt to *anyone*. The compulsion to rationalize is an *unnatural* "use of force" tactic; an unnatural force where self-generated deception is voluntarily chosen from a menu of alternatives.

In summary, cognitive dissonance activates a compulsion to confess or rationalize. Which one, depends on the offender's focus. Is the focus on the victim, or on self?

Every human desires the Crossroads.

Every human *wants* to feel guilt-free. Every human *needs* to feel guilt-free. The reason for wanting and needing to be guilt-free is the consequence of guilt; inner hell. Our beliefs are constantly tested. We are challenged to act in accordance with our beliefs, but the human condition includes falling to temptations. Acting contrary to personal beliefs is inevitable to some extent. No one is immune. When it happens, cognitive dissonance sets in, an inner conflict that tightens the guts more and more until it's resolved. Cognitive dissonance is part punishment and part alarm bell. It signals a need to change. Cognitive dissonance is consistent when we are inconsistent. When we act inconsistent with what we believe, cognitive dissonance will always go into action without fail. Cognitive dissonance consistently opens the gap between actions and beliefs, always resulting in a feeling of guilt.

The V-gap inner conflict is the result of focusing on the consequences and suffering of others instead of self, that is, the guilty person has low self-interest. This type of cognitive dissonance flips a switch. It activates a compulsion to confess as the only solution to resolving the inner conflict. When the V-gap is wide enough, the switch turns, compelling the offender to relieve inner pressure, stress, and anxiety with a true confession. This pressure relief closes the V-gap, moving the person to the Crossroad at the middle of the X.

A-gap causes exactly the same tension, stress, and anxiety… but with one difference. The cause is the offender's focus on personal consequences and suffering, that is, high self-interest. This perspective activates a compulsion to rationalize; to deceive through lies, alibis, and denials. Rationalization closes the A-gap, the same way that a true confession closes the V-gap and the result is the same: guilt-free, inner peace. The only difference is the duration. Reconciliation through true confession has a lasting effect for that wrongdoing. Reconciliation through rationalization doesn't last. It never lasts. It's only temporary. Cognitive dissonance will set in again. In other words, reaching the Crossroad through rationalization is never permanent. Inevitably, either the V-gap or A-gap will be re-opened.

The quest for the truth is a psychological battle between two feelings: pain, and pain-free. The natural state of truth-telling is predicated on a force of nature; the pain of guilt. Guilt is not pleasant. It's painful. Left unchecked, guilt can become a raging psychological hell, and a battle for the mind that results in a *war of words,* where words are used to relieve guilt one way or another. Getting the truth requires winning the war of words.

The difference between winning and losing the war of words is in triggering the *need* to feel guilt-free instead of *wanting* to feel guilt-free. The basic difference between *want* and *need* is *intensity* and *choice*. Wanting to feel guilt-free is negotiable. Wanting allows compromise. Need is different. Need is non-negotiable. Need gives no room for compromise. A need triggers a *self-generated performance demand* where only one solution is called up and called out. Want triggers a less intense response, such as scanning the menu and looking over alternatives to choose what is best under the circumstances, or, choose nothing at all. Want calls out a multiple choice selection. Need calls out just one decision, and it's a no-brainer decision.

Wrongdoings start a chain reaction, setting in motion a chain of traceable controllable or uncontrollable events; a series of intended or unintended consequences and outcomes depending on how bad we feel. The human quest to feel guilt-free is marked and marred with a continuum of offences. Contrary to popular belief, there are more than the two guarantees of paying taxes and death in life. Another one is the guarantee of doing wrong. Wrongdoing is part of human imperfection. Sinning is an unavoidable part of the good versus evil battle. Sins are not created equal. There are minor wrongdoings, and then there are major ones. The degree of wrong corresponds to the level of guilt, a scale of inner conflict that ranges from extremely low to extremely high. The level of guilt determines the reaction. *What is felt is determined by what is believed.*

The distinction between right and wrong is not created equal. It's a personalized belief, built and customized to what is uniquely learned and experienced. Our right-from-wrong belief builds individual moral standards, moral beliefs, and moral character. Moral reasoning is connected to worldview. How we view the world and the events that shape it is determined by what is learned and what is not learned, as well as what is experienced and what is not experienced. At the top of the list of experiences is consequence. The quantity and quality of consequences is directly linked to moral reasoning.

An interviewer's words can ethically and legally trigger cognitive dissonance. Response words, from the person being questioned, can relieve cognitive dissonance. The choice of words determines the direction on the X. The difference between winning the war of words is decisions. Every interview, every interaction intended to get the truth is predicated on decisions. Whether the truth is revealed or concealed depends on the decisions of words.

∞

CHAPTER 4
24 LAWS OF TRUTH: PRINCIPLES OF THE X THEORY OF TRUTH

There is no concrete blueprint that positively adds up to the truth. The truth is based on theory. Here are my 24 theoretical Laws of Truth, the fundamental principles on which the *X Theory of Truth* is based.

#1. If the truth hurts, you'll never get it.

If the truth hurts, if it causes inner pain, you will never get the truth, because *truth is a natural pain-reliever,* not a pain-inflictor. Lying is supposed to cause inner pain; if it becomes an inner pain-reliever, you'll never get the truth. Keep that in mind – literally. Keeping that in the offender's mind, and keeping it in your mind gets the truth. If that's not in either mind, the truth will not come out because it won't get called out.

The natural state of honesty and dishonesty builds equilibrium of inner pain and inner pain-relief. When the natural state exists, the truth reveals. However, the truth conceals when an unnatural state develops. If equilibrium becomes unbalanced by mixing up what causes and what relieves inner pain, the truth hides. It gets buried.

Getting a true confession boils down to pain and pleasure. When we tell the truth, we are supposed to feel the inner peace of being guilt-free, that is, harmony. The truth is supposed to set our soul free. The difference between succeeding and failing to get the truth is the extent of inner pain and inner pain-relief that the truth causes. The *X Theory of Truth* shows how to reach the natural state of honesty and dishonesty to get a true confession. The *X Theory of Truth* is an inner pain-management system intended to build honesty-dishonesty equilibrium so that what is supposed to be naturally felt will be felt.

#2. **The conscience is the most important force in getting the truth.**

The truth starts and finishes with the conscience. Don't look any farther. Don't look past the conscience. The conscience is the full solution to any problem surrounding the truth. The conscience is the starting line...but it's also the finish line.

Make the conscience work. Triple meaning – make it work out, make it work right, and make it do all the work. Strengthen the conscience, use its strength to execute flawlessly, and let a strong conscience do all the heavy lifting. Let the conscience lift the heavy weight of guilt.

A strong conscience activates a force of nature called the *compulsion to confess,* a natural conflict resolution that relieves the pain of inner hell caused by guilt and its companions: stress, anxiety, and pressure. Any focus other than on the conscience of who you want the truth from is a waste of time and energy, guaranteed to lead to frustration and failure.

#3. **The difference between revealing the truth and concealing it is the function of conscience.**

The *function of conscience* determines whether the truth is revealed or concealed. The function of conscience means how well the conscience works and works out. This results in two separate but connected concepts:
  i. Concept #1 - How well the conscience works determines whether the truth works out.
  ii. Concept #2 - How well the conscience works is determined by how well the conscience works out.

Concept #1: The truth doesn't just happen. The truth happens for a reason. It's worked out. The truth is the outcome of effort. That means it takes effort to activate the compulsion. The offender's conscience has to exert its strength to call out the truth. In some cases, no external appeal is necessary when the offender's conscience is strong enough to take care of all the work. In other cases, external appeal is needed. A lifting partner is needed. Someone has to help work out the truth.

Concept #2: A strong conscience doesn't just happen. It doesn't happen randomly, and it doesn't happen overnight. A strong conscience, like muscle, has to be worked out. No one is born with a strong conscience. It has to be built and then maintained through a *strength and conditioning program* that involves quality instruction combined with quality and quantity of REPS: **R**eal-life **E**xperience **P**roduces **S**trength. A team effort of coaching and mentoring has to teach the basics of moral character and ethical reasoning. Right from wrong has to be taught by the experts. Yet, knowing is never enough. Practice truly does make perfect. Real-life experience of exercising free will to make the tough moral calls is the only way to build upper-level strength of conscience.

Strength of character, moral strength, and ethical strength are all products of past strength and conditioning of the conscience. The frustration of failing to get the truth is the product of a wrong focus. Change the perspective of interviewing to a strength and conditioning program. Changing the focus changes the outcome. Strengthen the person's conscience. Make the conscience work out to work out the truth.

#4. Make the conscience work right. A truly functional conscience will never be denied, and will never deny.

Functional conscience reveals the truth. *Dysfunctional* conscience conceals the truth. A functional conscience is an unstoppable force. It will force the truth to reveal to *someone*. It may be you or someone else, but a functional conscience will not be denied, and will not deny.

A strong conscience will work right. That means flawless execution. A strong conscience will work its hardest to do what's right by not being denied and never denying the truth. Denials don't just happen. They are the result of conscious decision-making stemming directly from a weak, undeveloped, dysfunctional conscience.

#5. Failure to get the truth is caused by malfunction.

Malfunction is the leading cause of truth concealment. A malfunctioning conscience cannot and will not activate the compulsion to confess. A malfunctioning conscience is too weak to lift the heavy weight of guilt.

The leading cause of malfunction is the wrong focus; the offender and the interviewer are focused on the wrong consequences of the wrongdoing. The wrong focus weakens a strong conscience, and makes a weak consequence dysfunctional. *What you focus on grows.* Focusing on the suffering of victim and others makes high cognitive dissonance grow. It opens V-gap, widening it until the compulsion to confess is activated. Focusing on the offender's consequences and suffering makes low cognitive dissonance grow. It opens A-gap, widening it until the compulsion to rationalize is activated.

#6. A strong conscience has limitless lifting capacity.

There's no limit to the truth you can get from a person with a strong conscience. A strong conscience, in top shape, will do all the work, all the heavy lifting by lifting the crushing weight of guilt.

#7. The conscience is continuously subject to atrophy and hypertrophy.

Atrophy is the weakening of the conscience. Hypertrophy is the strengthening of the conscience. The bad news is that a strong conscience can atrophy without working out. A strong conscience can get into miserably bad shape. Even worse news is that you, the person conducting the interview, can be responsible for atrophy by losing the war of words.

The good news is that an atrophied conscience can be built-up by winning the war of words with a great interview. You can be responsible for conscience-hypertrophy with the right communication. What you say and how you say it has an anabolic or catabolic effect on strength of conscience.

#8. **The myth of "no conscience" is the strongest limiting belief in the truth-seeking process.**

"He has no conscience" is a myth. It's a false, misleading statement. If you're alive…you have a conscience. Every human has a conscience. No exceptions. The only issue about a conscience is its strength. Is it lean and mean, or soft and weak? Is the conscience strong, developed, and functional, or fragile, under-development, and dysfunctional? "He has no conscience" is slang for "he has a weak conscience", or "he has a dysfunctional conscience." It means that work is needed to get the truth because, like a muscle, a conscience can get stronger or weaker depending on training and use.

Believing that "he has no conscience" is true is an excuse for not getting the truth. It's a limiting belief that gets in the way of getting the truth. The first step in becoming an expert at getting the truth is eliminating the myth from your thought process and vocabulary. Once you've deleted the myth from your thinking, you have eliminated a limiting belief. You've just raised the bar.

#9. **You can't hide from your conscience. You can only lower the bar.**

What is a conscience? I use two definitions; a philosophical one, and a spiritual definition. There's a common thread that unites both definitions: the conscience is an inner voice that judges performance. But not all inner voices are created equal. Some are louder, persistent, and deadly accurate. Others are barely audible. Everyone is born with a conscience, but no one is born with a strong conscience. A strong conscience is built. It's developed. The same applies to a weak conscience. Here is the philosophical definition of conscience: the super-ego.

Sigmund Freud theorized that the human personality is composed of the id, the ego, and the super-ego.[2] The id and the ego are diametrically opposed polar opposites that play games through a lot of fighting inside our minds. The super-ego is the conscience; the judge that referees the fight by sending feelings of peace or guilt that reward or punish.

The id is our inner child, governed by the *pleasure principle*. The id is driven by an extraordinary need for instant gratification. It wants it all and it wants it right now. No struggle, no pain, and no delay. The id is impulsive, impatient, and immature. The id is not in touch with reality.

The ego is the id's opponent. It's the part of our personality that is in touch with reality. The ego is governed by the *reality principle*, that is, rewards are not instant. Rewards are the product of blood, sweat, tears, struggle, hard work, and most of all, disappointments.

The clash of the id and the ego not only plays mind games, it represents the fight for our mind, our personality, and our character. The id is a head-case. The ego tries to change the id. Good versus evil. Entitlement versus earned. The dark side versus the bright side. The ego tries to control the out-of-control id. The side that wins the battle determines personality. The difference between winning and losing the character war is how well the ego gets built. A weak ego is no match for the id's wild-side. An underdeveloped ego loses out to the id every time. But a strong, well-built ego always beats the id. A well-built ego doesn't just happen. No one is born with a well-developed ego. It's built with intense training and experience that learns a socially-accepted, realistic means to getting the prize. In other words, building a well-built ego takes hard work to *mature*. Maturity takes a team effort; parents, teachers, relatives, friends, and every element of the true social networking…not the artificial one on your screen.

---

2   From Sigmund Freud's 1920 essay, "Beyond the Pleasure Principle" first published in German.

The super-ego is Freud's version of the conscience. It's the inner voice that scores the ego's performance with feeling. The super-ego/conscience rewards moral behaviour with guilt-free inner peace, and punishes immorality with guilt, stress, and anxiety. However, a healthy super-ego doesn't just happen either. It needs to get right from wrong straight. A strong conscience has to deeply comprehend the true meaning of right from wrong in order to score the fight properly.

There's a synonym for an id-oriented person – an asshole. An immature, self-centered, self-absorbed amateur who cannot see past one's self because of a blinding spotlight shining intensely on that same one's self.

An ego-oriented person is conscientious; a mature professional who know what it takes to get it done. The difference between an id-oriented and ego-oriented person is the interest-rate. The ego-oriented have low self-interest. Id-oriented have off-the-chart high self-interest.

How well the super-ego/conscience does its job depends on blood guts, that is, clearly knowing the difference between right from wrong in your blood and the guts to not lower the bar.

#10. What's the difference between conscience and soul?

Reaching a spiritual definition of conscience needs a comparison – what's the difference between conscience and soul? I asked the experts, religious leaders, and I've been told the same answer, and it's confusing, but I gave it a shot anyway.

Our *soul* is a piece of God that lives for eternity. The body dies, but the soul won't. The soul gives us a mission that will keep trying to reveal itself no matter what we do to stop it. Our soul is a power source and our connection to the Highest Power, driven to have its goodness remain untainted from the forces of evil. The soul is our connection to our Personal Coach who directs us toward what needs to be done. There are two forces that get in the way: evil and free will. Evil has one goal: to stop our soul's mission. Our job is to protect our soul with a viscous defense, and attack evil with a relentless offense that goes as deep as possible. Free will is our ability to make the right call, to make the right move even when we can't see three moves ahead. Evil is a misleader encouraging us to make the wrong call by dressing it up as the right call. Evil tries to change our soul's intended direction by persuading, dissuading, and betraying with smooth closing arguments, trying to prove that the truth is false. Evil constantly attempts to raise reasonable doubt to darken overwhelming evidence.

The *conscience* is our inner judge that dishes out corrective punishment for moral ineptitude, and rewards moral competence. The conscience is the soul's communication director. The conscience does not work independently. The conscience has a boss: the soul. The soul is too busy trying to lift us, so it delegates the managerial communication responsibilities to the conscience to prevent the soul from breaking its focus.

The conscience is the voice of your soul, coaching you, correcting you, and rewarding you, speaking straight from the heart; honesty out and honesty in. The conscience makes sure that the soul is heard. The soul is our pulse. It's what makes us tick. The conscience protects the soul, trying to keep it strong, and prevent us from weakening it.

However, there's something else special about the soul. The soul accomplishes what nature and nurture can't explain. The soul defies conventional thinking. The soul makes things happen that can't be inherited and can't be woman-made. The soul is not artificial or superficial – it's deep. The soul is our personal mystery, a life's work to discover our truth. The soul works its wonders when we need someone, and when someone needs us. Someone always will need you, and we will always need someone. Needing someone flips the switch, which is a call to action for the soul to work its magic. How we respond to who needs us determines what happens inside. We reveal and heal our soul by how we respond to the call. The soul has a motto: need it and demand it. When the soul makes a lifting demand, there's no option but to comply. Trying to avoid that responsibility calls the conscience into action. Then the noise starts, and it gets louder until we follow instructions. Eventually, that's how the truth reveals. Truth reveals because we supply what's demanded by our conscience.

#11. The compulsion to confess is an unstoppable force of nature.

Do you have trouble keeping a secret? Have you ever confided in someone and immediately regretted it, wondering why in the world you spilled your guts? If you think there's something dragging it out, forcing you to talk out of control about private matters, you're right; it's not your imagination. There's a force inside us that makes us tell the truth. It's called the *compulsion to confess*.

Theodore Reik, a Freudian psychiatrist, pioneered the theoretical concept of the compulsion to confess.[3] Reik theorized that every person has the urge to tell the truth as a solution to the inner conflict brought on by wrongdoings. We all have a potentially unstoppable force that pushes out a confession to mediate transgressions when our id and ego do battle over gratification – the war over instant and delayed gratification. The compulsion to confess is the conscience/super-ego's conflict management strategy to reconcile the id's perspective of impulsivity. A confession is intended to change future perspective from the pleasure of immediate gratification to the pain of the impulsivity that causes it. The urge to confess is the inner correctional services at works. The conscience uses a confession to correct conduct that is internalized as wrong.

Like the conscience itself, the strength of the compulsion to confess varies. The urge to confess fluctuates. It can be strengthened

---

[3] Theodore Reik (1959). The Compulsion to Confess. Grove Press, New York.

or weakened depending on the direction of the cognitive dissonance. A focus on victim suffering strengthens the compulsion to confess. When the focus shifts to personal consequences suffered by the offender, the compulsion to confess weakens, replaced by the compulsion to rationalize.

The compulsion to confess has one mission: to teach us that the reality of ego-driven strategies will steer us in the right direction. The ego is the part of our personality that deals in reality. The ego teaches us that we can't get everything we want overnight. The ego is the inner mentor that coaches us to understand the concept of struggle in association with achievement. The id is the work-aversion part of our personality. The id believes in entitlement, not earning and reward.

#12. Cognitive dissonance rips open a gap that can tear apart.

Have you ever felt like hell when you do "too much" of what you know is not good for you? Too much food, too much booze, too much whining, too much complaining, too much gossiping, too much backstabbing, too much waste of time and energy, loafing around? Have you ever felt like hell when you underachieve?

If you do, you're suffering from cognitive dissonance. The good news is it's curable. The bad news is that cold cases raise the temperature; unsolved cognitive dissonance will turn into a raging inner hell.

Cognitive dissonance opens a gap on the top or the bottom of the X. Any distance between your moral beliefs and your conduct rips opens a gap. Our conscience works diligently to close the gap because, deep down, we all prefer the Crossroad, the middle of the X where actions and conduct cross together in perfect alignment.

Every human has an inner motor that works to achieve inner peace, especially when cognitive dissonance sets in…which happens often. Being human means spending a considerable amount of time fighting cognitive dissonance. Life is a vicious cycle of opening gaps and closing them.

#13. A person's right-from-wrong score directly relates to a willingness and capacity to tell the truth.

I've spent my entire adult life teaching student-athletes the difference between right and wrong using football and weight lifting to educate about a wide range of issues. The majority of rookies scored low on any sort of test. I've learned four lessons about moral education:

i. What is obviously wrong is not obvious.
ii. Many define wrong wrongly.
iii. The reason for #1 & #2 above is wrong training – wrong instruction and an ass-backward system of rewards and corrections.
iv. Even lost causes can find the true meaning of right with the right training.

The low score of right from wrong has never been an intentional mindset in students. It's a result of what they've been taught, what they haven't been taught, what they've learned, and what they have not learned. What they process becomes hardwired. I learned that change can be effected with a three-step process. I start by spelling out right from wrong. I hand out a written list of prohibited conducts that are concretely defined as wrong. Secondly, I teach and preach the same list; relentlessly. But the true test is practice. Moral reps. Doing the right thing over and over changes the wiring. It can be done.

Moral character is directly connected to the willingness and capacity to tell the truth, because the high or low score determines whether the compulsion to confess is activated easily or not. The phrase "moral character" automatically brings to mind preaching or sermons. That's not correct. Moral character is an outcome of what we believe and what we do. Moral character is directly linked to cognitive dissonance – whether cognitive dissonance is actually suffered, how much, and for how long.

In its simplest form, strong moral character is not sainthood. It starts with a healthy understanding of what is right and what is wrong, and it's measured by how close the true definition of moral character is flawlessly executed. No one scores a perfect 10, but there's an expectation to score high. The problem with defining and classifying right from wrong is that the definition is an abstract concept open to multiple interpretations. There's considerable debate about what heading to put certain behaviour under. What we define as wrong depends largely on past reps – what we've been taught, what we've learned, what we've forgotten, what we've internalized, and what we've practiced.

The success of every interview depends on the suspect's definition of right and wrong. You can't activate a suspect's compulsion to confess without the suspect scoring high on the right-from-wrong test. The suspect's definition of right-from-wrong determines the extent of cognitive dissonance suffered…if at all.

The good news is that you can raise the suspect's score by teaching him the true meaning of wrong and the true severity of the wrong he committed. The bad news is time restrictions. You haven't got months, or weeks, or days. You have a few hours, or even minutes. The key is to make the biggest impact in the shortest amount of time by not wasting words. You can't kill valuable time off the clock with wasted plays. Every word must have relevance, meaning, and purpose, but most importantly, it has to be *straight from the heart;* the only words that work in any interview.

#14. Heart-to-heart is the only way to build a rapport strong enough to make an impact.

Contrary to popular belief, interview strategy is not the most important factor in getting the truth. What you say is, of course, important, but *how* you say it matters most. Nothing matters more than the manner of communication, because *how* you communicate either *builds* rapport or *destroys* it.

Rapport is a bond that helps bind the conscience to tell the truth. The truth will never be told without rapport. The compulsion to confess will never activate without rapport. The conscience doesn't respond without rapport. Rapport is the essential plug-in that stimulates the conscience.

The key is to define what *is* and what *is not* rapport. Let's start with what is not. Rapport isn't a buddy relationship. It isn't a social connection by sending a friend request, or accepting one, or pressing "like" to juvenile posts, or chatting mindlessly through cyberspace. Rapport is not winning a popularity contest. Rapport is not about approval. Rapport is not about being liked. Rapport is a heart-to-heart connection that sends a message that is believed. You're a professional. You're not a bungling amateur, you're not a bullshitter, or an asshole or a punk. In other words, you're not a liar, or a hater, or an over-officious bully, but you will not take any shit. You're not an enabling pushover, and you know exactly what you're doing. You can be trusted. When you develop rapport with who you're interviewing, you've earned the highest credibility score, that is, confidence in competence.

In some cases, the suspect is familiar with you. In some cases, he's a total stranger. Either way, you need to score high on the credibility rating in the suspect's mind. There's only one way to do it: straight-from-the-heart communication. It's the only kind of communication that speaks heart-to-heart. Straight-from-the-heart communication prevents miscommunication, and guarantees 100% accurate translation.

Straight-from-the-heart communication is not one kind of voice tone or specific body language. It's communication that achieves two objectives:
    i.   Reveals true self.
    ii.   Strikes a chord.

You have to have presence by revealing your true self and by hitting a nerve.

The two biggest interview mistakes are *artificiality* and *superficiality*:
  i. Concealing true self behind artificial layers of confusion.
  ii. Words bouncing off the suspect with superficial language that is unwilling and incapable of going deep.

#15. The compulsion to rationalize is a stoppable force of nature.

"Life's too short."

Those three words may be the easiest and most common rationalization to justify doing too much of what's not good for us. It's just one example of the infinite excuses we concoct to justify bone-headedness, or being an asshole, or laziness, or incompetence, or flat-out immorality.

The *compulsion to rationalize* shares one element with the compulsion to confess: both are pain-relievers. They both relieve cognitive dissonance. They both close gaps and reach the Crossroad of guilt-free inner peace. Yet, there's one glaring difference: rationalization is temporary pain relief. A band-aid solution. It never sticks.

Both compulsions are switches that trigger response. Both switches are activated by pressure, but the type of pressure decides which switch is pressed. The pressure of focusing on the victim's suffering presses the compulsion-to-confess switch. The pressure of focusing on personal consequences and suffering presses the compulsion-to-rationalize switch.

From an interviewer's perspective, a suspect's rationalization may be frustrating, but in reality, it will work in your favour by helping you get the truth eventually. Rationalization never cures cognitive dissonance. It only masks the pain. Once the band-aid rips off, the pain gets worse. Rationalization only adds fuel to the inner hell. Self-deception is self-inflicted pressure. Lies and alibis always turn up the inner heat. Rationalization never fails to raise the inner conflict to a boiling point, a wide V-gap that activates and strengthens the compulsion to confess to the maximum, forcing the deceiver to tell someone the truth

#16. All rationalization is a step down the ladder.

"Bullshit baffles brains."

I heard that for the first time on my second day as a rookie cop. I didn't see the dual meaning at the time. The obvious meaning is that the deceiver *may* confuse the receiver with fiction if the receiver is gullible enough. But the second meaning wasn't immediately obvious. The deceiver *will* confuse his/her own mind when the weight of his/her own bullshit becomes too heavy to carry.

Every rationalized justification changes the mind by taking a step down the ladder. Here's what it means: The top of the V-gap in the "X" diagram is the highest you can go on the moral ladder. When the conscience activates and strengthens the compulsion to confess resulting in a self-generated true confession, moral character is at the top of its game. However, when the A-gap is closed at the bottom of the X by rationalizing, a step is taken down the moral ladder. Another A-gap is formed beneath it, representing a lower step on the moral ladder. Every lower step changes the person's definition of right and wrong. Every lower step represents a lower moral standard, a different and more skewed perspective of right-from-wrong.

As the ladder's size increases with more and more lower steps, the road to the top gets tougher and tougher. Every lower step weakens the conscience and weakens the compulsion to confess. The switch gets less and less sensitive. The bad news is that all the bullshit that builds more lower steps will baffle the person's own brains, obscuring his/her original belief of right and wrong. The good news is that the ladder can be climbed through re-training. Words can have a lifting effect when they are carefully aimed, reaching the conscience and re-wiring the mess created by piled-up bullshit. Getting through to a baffled mind is not easy…but great accomplishments are never easy.

#17. The bigger the crime, the wider the gap.

CASE STUDY #2

I was assigned to investigate a homicide after a skeleton was found in a field. The victim had been reported missing for a long time. Not much to work on with only a few leads. The case was seemingly a lost cause. Then we interviewed just about everyone in the community. Twenty-two people, including two of the suspect's girlfirends, told us the suspect had implicated himself in statements to them. In other words, there were twenty-two confessions to persons *not* in authority (persons who were not police officers).

Why did the suspect tell 22 people? Bad case of cognitive dissonance. An extremely wide V-gap activated the compulsion to confess over and over, meaning we probably missed a few people. Lesson learned: the severity of the crime is connected to the compulsion to confess. The more severe the crime, the harder it is for the suspect to keep it a secret. The more severe the crime, the wider the V-gap; the wider the V-gap, the stronger the compulsion to confess…to anyone. A fully activated compulsion to confess that forced the suspect to tell 22 people can't be easily shut off. After he was arrested, the suspect gave us a true confession. It was natural. The next time you fail to get a true confession, interview the suspect's inner circle or who he/she meets. You'll likely find a true confession to a person *not* in authority.

Why did 22 people tell the truth and implicate him? Bad case of cognitive dissonance. Hiding the truth about a human being's death caused extreme inner hell. Exactly half of the 22 witnesses didn't like the police. They started with a bad attitude. Some even hurled insults. But rapport was built. How? Don't take it personal, don't make it personal. The focus was changed to the victim and *potential victims* – the suspect was still loose; literally and figuratively. Changing the focus changed the outcome.

The *power of extreme cognitive dissonance* is a major investigative advantage in major crime investigations. Nothing stimulates the conscience more than the thought of innocent people suffering extremely. Nothing activates and strengthens the compulsion to tell the truth more than extreme wrong. Nothing brings out the very best in people than the extreme worst. Nothing brings out what's right than extreme wrong.

Unlike "obviously wrong," no one has to explain to anyone that extreme wrong is wrong. The only obstruction that prevents understanding extreme wrong is a loss of sanity. No one can rationalize extreme wrong. Trying to justify extreme wrong won't work out. It's the equivalent of a wasted time out in football.

From an interviewer's perspective, the natural effect of extreme wrong works to your truth-seeking benefit if you *stick to the right focus*. What you focus on grows. What you don't focus on doesn't grow.

#18. The myth of "He won't talk" is unnatural. The Process brings out the natural.

"He won't talk."

I heard that so many times inside police stations that I lost count. I never understood it then, and I don't understand it now. I've always believed it was a concession, a forfeit instead of trying. I fully understand that winning and losing may not be the politically correct way of viewing truth-seeking, but it's the truth. The truth is a win, lies are a loss. Getting the truth is your job. It's the objective of every investigation. It's the central core function of justice. Fiction is for entertainment.

I've always believed that the true translation for *"He won't talk"* is *"I don't want to try."* It's a rationalization, and a justification for not trying.

"He's been through the system. He won't say anything."

More rationalization, and more justification for not trying.

It's unnatural to "not want to talk." The compulsion to confess doesn't mysteriously disappear. It gets weak and out of shape, but the potential is still there. It's always there, but just hidden. Buried. Even if you fail to get the truth, the attempt will take a major step to getting the truth. It will strengthen the compulsion to confess so that he/she will later confess to someone else…a person *not* in authority. You may not activate the compulsion to confess, but strengthening it is a major achievement. You may not press the switch, but you start the process of putting some natural pressure on the switch.

Activating the compulsion to confess takes a *process*. The interviewer is only a part of the process. The process includes every other person in the suspect's life. That's the reason why some people tell the truth right away with minimal interview effort, why people tell the truth after a lot of interview effort, why some people lie, and why others say nothing at all. But every interview, regardless of the outcome, effects change. All it takes is some effort.

#19. "Appealing to the conscience" is a misleading phrase. It's slang for "strengthening the conscience's compulsion to confess."

"Appealing to the conscience" doesn't build the right interviewing mindset. The word *"appeal"* means to make a plea, or make a request for help. That's not how the conscience works. The conscience is a use of force that compels the truth. The conscience doesn't need pleas to ask someone to please tell the truth. The conscience only needs to be strengthened. When it's strong enough, the rest happens *naturally*. A strong conscience activates the compulsion to confess. No appeal is needed.

Changing the focus from *appeal to strengthen* changes the outcome. It changes the interviewing mindset by shifting the focus to working *with* the conscience as opposed to working *on* the conscience, that is, to get the conscience to do what it does naturally. The change of focus is the key to making the right interview *decisions* to select interview language and communication *instinctively* and *intuitively* from a structured *system*, the equivalent of calling the right play from a playbook through a natural rapid decision-making process.

#20. Decision-making is one of the most over-looked and under-rated elements of interviewing.

Every interview is a series of decisions. Decisions have to be made at warp-speed during an interview – decisions about what to say, what *not* to, and how to say it. The success or failure of every interview depends on the quality of decisions made. Decision-making skills don't just happen. They're developed over time. "Winging it" won't work. Scripting it won't work. The solution is systematic strategizing & improvising.

A system is a limitless playbook made up of a *decision-making model* and *concepts*, the building blocks of a professional dialogue. Concepts are not scripts that are mechanically memorized and robotically recalled. Scripts are not straight from the heart; they don't build heart-to-heart rapport. Concepts are strategies that are pieced together for one purpose: to strengthen the compulsion to confess. A decision-making model teaches and guides the most difficult interview skill of all: deciding on the next call.

The biggest challenge of any interview is unpredictability. It is impossible to forecast with certainty how a suspect will respond to your dialogue. The difference between a successful and failed interview is the speed and quality of interview decisions. Nothing else matters. The solution is the decision-making principle of *strategizing* & improvising; make a general plan with structured adaptation to fit the situation.

Without a general plan, an interview is guaranteed to fail. A rigid plan also guarantees failure. The objective of general planning is building a *framework of concepts*; frame a message and decide on concepts that fit the specific interview situation. General planning aims at the *expected* – creating it and responding to it. Improvisation solves the *unexpected*. It's the expertise of making the right call from the system to adapt to the unexpected.

Strategizing & improvising guarantees *natural* communication. The natural process of the conscience responds only to natural communication.

#21. The main reason why people lie to you is their high tolerance to inner pain.

To become an expert at getting the truth, you have to become an expert at why people lie to you.

Inner pain management is the key issue in truth-telling. If you can handle the level of inner pain caused by your cognitive dissonance, you will lie. If you can't take it, you'll tell the truth. Your pain threshold is directly related to the exchange-rate. What will you get in exchange for the truth? More pain, or pain relief?

Pain tolerance to lying skyrockets when certain conditions exist. Here is the list of conditions that guarantee you will be lied to:

i. Wrong focus. If the interview focuses on the suspect's consequences, expect to be lied to.
ii. Fear that intended outcome won't happen. The intended outcome is the middle of the X – guilt-free inner peace. If the suspect suspects you will prevent that feeling, you will be lied to.
iii. Low credibility score. All human interaction involves credibility evaluation. If the suspect believes you are a bungling amateur, or a fool, or untrustworthy, or a flat-out asshole, you will be lied to.
iv. Poor conditioning. Compulsive liars aren't born. They're made. Rewards and reinforcement are the anabolic agents of lying. Compulsive lying is hardwired by REPS – **R**epeated **E**nabling **P**roduces **S**torytellers. Chronic enabling fuels habitual lying. Deceivers are conditioned to lie when they believe that they repeatedly *benefit* from lying. Enablers

are those who let it slide by turning their heads intentionally or unintentionally to the person's lies. You will be lied to when the suspect believes it will pay off. That happens when they lump you together with all their past enablers. In other words, you will be lied to when the suspect is conditioned to believe that s/he will be believed.
   v.   All of the above.

Preventing these conditions prevents being lied to.

#22. The main reason people tell you the truth is low tolerance to inner pain.

People tell you the truth when their inner pain tolerance bottoms out. When they are sensitive to the pain of inner hell, you will be told the truth. Here are five reasons that explain how it happens:

i. Right focus. If the interview focuses on the suffering of others, expect the truth.

ii. No fear that intended outcome will happen. The intended outcome is the middle of the X – guilt-free inner peace. If the suspect is fully convinced he can escape inner hell, and that inner peace will be achieved, expect the truth.

iii. High credibility score. If the suspect takes you seriously by respecting your ability and integrity, expect the truth.

iv. Top-level conditioning. If the suspect believes you are different than the cheerleaders who have rewarded his/her lying and made him a career deceiver, and if you're not lumped together with all the enablers in his/her life, expect the truth. When the suspect can't see the potential benefit of lying because you won't accept it, you will be told the truth.

v. All of the above.

#23. Honesty out, honesty in.

Everyone is an expert at picking out a liar, because lying is not uncommon. Lying is not a rarity. In all likelihood, it's probably unlikely to go through one day without being lied to. Key to interviewing expertise is honesty out, honesty in.

The power of honesty attracts honesty. The power of dishonesty attracts dishonesty. Honesty and dishonesty are both sources of energy. One cleans the environment while the other contaminates the environment. Honesty can't get through poison.

The top trait in becoming an expert truth-receiver goes far beyond interview and interrogation technique. The number-one characteristic is being a *lifter; solve more problems than you cause. Relieve more pain than you inflict.* This is the definition of success, in whatever you do professionally or personally. It's impossible to succeed at anything by causing more problems than you solve. It's impossible to lead or follow by inflicting more pain that you relieve.

#24. It's easier to get the truth than to be lied to.

Getting lied to takes work. It's unnatural exertion. Getting the truth is easier, because it's natural. To summarize, you have four forces of nature going in your favour to get the truth. By nature, humans:
    i.   Suffer cognitive dissonance.
    ii.   Try to eliminate it.
    iii. Use a confession to do it.
    iv. Have a compulsion to confess that forces it out of them.

The suspect has everything it takes to work with you to get a true confession.

∞

To be continued in Book 2…

Enjoy the book?
We would like to hear from you.

Post a review on Amazon, Goodreads or let us know directly at reviews@ginoarcaro.com.

Follow Gino on Social Media

GinoArcaro

@Gino_Arcaro

+GinoArcaro

GinoArcaro

Gino's Blog

Follow Jordan Publications Inc. on Social Media
for up-to-the-minute information on Gino and his books

GinoArcaro.Author

@JordanPubInc

+GinoArcaroBooks

More Books by Gino Arcaro

Soul of a Lifter
Gino Arcaro's journey from childhood obesity to natural health and strength was not made alone; he relied on the Soul of a Lifter. In telling this tale, Arcaro draws on life lessons learned from his careers as a football coach, police officer and college teacher to inspire and lead the reader in a soul-searching quest to reach his/her own potential. This is not your run-of-the-mill motivational book. Discover insights about what drives the soul… what happens when you listen and when you don't!

Selling H.E.L.L. in Hell
from the series Soul of an Entrepreneur
You may be starting out in business or just contemplating making the big decision. Gino Arcaro knows what you're thinking and wants to make sure you know what you're not thinking. His thought-bending tales, while entertaining and steeped in reality, will make the would-be business owner take a second and third look at the situation before jumping in. And, for those already "self-employed," Arcaro offers a unique slant on dealing with day-to-day customer and employee challenges.

eXplode: X Fitness Training System
Sought after his entire adult life to help others achieve their workout goals, Arcaro put his weight lifting theories and routines into this manual. His "Case Studies," true stories from his 40+ years of working out (completely natural) bring a sense of reality to the average gym-goer who just wants to get in shape, stay in shape, and most-importantly, not quit. No gimmicks, just discussion and formulas that can be tailored to any situation regardless of how long or how intensely one has been working out.

4th & Hell Season 1

"We were David with a Canadian passport, failing miserably at winning just one football game against stars-and-stripes-draped Goliaths." It came down to fourth and hell – a face-to-face showdown. No disguises, no masks, no secret weapons. No one huddled on the sideline. No one huddled on the field. Both sides knew what to expect. No surprises, no guess-work, no mind games. Making the call was a formality. All that mattered was running the play to see what would pass. Someone would execute; someone would be executed.

Fat Losing: The psychology of fat fighting
"Waste Mis-management leads to Waist Mis-management"

This is not a diet book. This 40-page eBook explains the most important truth about fighting fat: it begins at the top – literally. Without a proper mindset, no amount of dieting or counting calories will workout. Digesting Fat Losing is the first step to understanding how to change your habits and thinking for once and for all. It contains practical discussions that engage the reader in re-thinking the obstacles that stand in the way of becoming a healthier person. Gino Arcaro, a self-proclaimed "dysfunctional 12-year-old, trying to overcome my obesity," is an expert on the subject. He's written Fat Losing to share what he has learned and practiced for over 40 years.

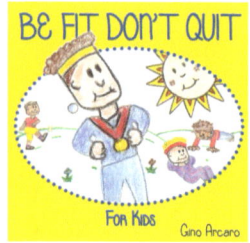

Be Fit Don't Quit

Full of exercise ideas young children can try on their own or with a parent, this book will rekindle in any adult a love for the simple act of playing. Gino Arcaro has spent his life working out and teaching young adults about the importance of "being fit." He wrote Be Fit Don't Quit to express a tried-and-true message: Exercising is natural and fun. Never quit!

SWAT Offense

By connecting partial concepts that can build any formation, any pass play and any running play to fit the situation, at the line of scrimmage, Arcaro has designed a system that eliminates the need for a conventional playbook that has to be memorized. Memorization is replaced by translation of a simple language. He designed the SWAT offense as a solution to a nightmarish reality of limitations – poor talent and poor resources, a one-man coaching staff, open-admission players, and on top of it all, out-matched opponents…willingly sought out! David constantly calling out Goliath. Arcaro's SWAT offense is the most unique offensive system you'll ever see because it has limitless offense capacity but no playbook. A unique feature of the SWAT Offense is its ties to SWAT Defense.

SWAT Defense

Making the defensive call has never been harder. Coordinators have the greatest challenges in football history. Spread no-huddle offenses, extreme passing, clock-changing rules. More to defend, less time to think. Arcaro's SWAT Defense shows how to beat the spread by forcing the offense to go deep and crack under pressure. "A stress-filled workplace for quarterbacks and receivers leads to an explosion." Central to Arcaro's system is his decision-making model that teaches defensive coordinators and players to make the right calls – those split-second decisions that have to be made about 60 times per game. Making the right call is not easy. Like any skill, defensive decision-makers need guidelines and experience to develop into full potential. A unique feature of the SWAT Defense is its ties to Arcaro's SWAT Offense.

For more free book previews or to purchase Gino's books go to
WWW.GINOARCARO.COM